I0824291

LIKE A RAINBOW

The Colorful Story of Cyndi Lauper

written by
Amy Guglielmo and Jacqueline Tourville
illustrated by Brigette Barrager

atheneum
Atheneum Books for Young Readers
New York Amsterdam/Antwerp London Toronto Sydney/Melbourne New Delhi

In Ozone Park, Queens, in the 1960s,
in a house as bright as a candy box,
lived a big Italian family . . .
and a little girl named Cyndi.

Cyndi wasn't just different—she was unusual.
She sang before she could talk,
and she never stopped!

While other kids followed the rules . . .
Cyndi was loud.
She was creative.
She was fearless.
Cyndi colored outside the lines.

Cyndi didn't mind that she stood out.

She had to be bold like a rainbow
and use her one-of-a-kind voice to be heard.
She had to let her true self shine.

Life in Cyndi's family was a roller coaster. There was worry, but there was also laughter . . . and lots of music.

Cyndi and her mother sang along to show tunes.
Her older sister, Ellen, taught her how to play guitar.

At twelve, Cyndi started writing her own songs,
which she performed for her nana and their neighbor Mrs. Schnur.
Sometimes, she sang too loud for their tastes.

Cyndi loved traveling to Manhattan to watch plays and visit museums. Her family couldn't afford to see Broadway shows, but someday, Cyndi would make it there!

She just didn't know how or when.

MATH
History

In high school, Cyndi dreamed in rhythms and songs, but she flunked English class.

Cyndi loved to dance, but she failed gym class.

Cyndi had style! She made her own clothes, but she dropped out of art class.

And when Cyndi shimmered and sang through the street, other kids threw rocks at her.

Then things happened in Cyndi's life that made her feel small and silent. When she was seventeen, Cyndi left home.

Her family knew she'd have important things to say. But no one else could show her the way.

So, Cyndi set out to find it. . . . *What you gonna do with your life?*

She wasn't sure what came next, but as she gazed over the rooftops of Queens, Cyndi saw a rainbow peeking through the clouds.

She followed its brightness and hope to her sister, Ellen.

Ellen gave Cyndi a couch to sleep on, Nana's spaghetti, and lots of love.

With time, Cyndi was able to heal.

One day a stray dog followed Cyndi home. Cyndi knew what it was like to feel lost and lonely, so she took the pup in and named her Sparkle. Sparkle followed Cyndi everywhere.

Cyndi tried settling back in Queens, but she was still a square peg in a round hole. She tried giving school another chance, but she failed every course. She tried looking for a job, but she didn't know what she could be.

Cyndi felt *hopeless*.

Then, under the rumbling platform of an elevated train, Cyndi's luck changed. Dazzling paintings caught her eye. They shouted: *Wake up!*

And then she saw a sign:

Her instructor, Bob, taught Cyndi how to paint and encouraged her to keep finding her true self. He suggested an art program in Canada . . . a long way from Queens.

But Cyndi didn't let the distance stop her. She packed up Sparkle and her art supplies and headed north!

In her new class, Cyndi sketched in a quiet forest, away from the city noise. In nature, she heard songs among the trees and found space to thrive. And she saw rainbows everywhere.

Cyndi was no longer a misfit. She had found her people.
She was an artist. She was a poet.
She was a singer and musician.

Cyndi could use art to express her true self . . .
but where would she do this?

Broke and hungry, she didn't want to be in New York.
And she didn't want to live on her sister's couch.
So she *drove all night*. . . .

Until she found herself in the Green Mountains of Vermont. The lush hills reminded her of the freedom she'd found in Canada.

Cyndi lived in a hostel for runaways—a safe place where kids could go if they'd left home—and met other teens who had faced big problems.

Cyndi was figuring out her own life, but she also wanted to help people. She got a job working in a kennel, and when she moved into an apartment, Cyndi made sure there was always room for teens who needed a place to stay—and a bowl of Nana's spaghetti.

Cyndi passed her high school exams, but she didn't have enough money to finish her college degree.

Once again, she packed up, grabbed Sparkle, and headed back to New York. . . .

She tried being a waitress, but she couldn't remember the orders.

She tried being a secretary, but she wasn't great at spelling.

She tried being a horse walker, but the workers at the track told her to *scram*!

Time after time, Cyndi tried on all kinds of jobs, but they never showed her *true colors*.

After trying everyone else's way of doing things, Cyndi realized she should shine in her own way. . . . She had to mix her art with her music.

Cyndi dyed her hair bright red. She dressed like a rainbow and wore layers of jangly jewelry. She painted the soles of her shoes to look like the places she'd lived. Cyndi wanted to be seen, she wanted to be heard, and she wanted to make a difference.

She wrote new songs and performed on the street for money.
Cyndi sang her heart out.

At first, just her colorful hair and wild clothes grabbed people's attention.
But when Cyndi sang her feelings with her marvelous voice, she got noticed!

Soon, Cyndi joined a band, but they weren't very good. People booed and threw things at the stage, just like the kids had thrown rocks at Cyndi years ago.

Cyndi wasn't singing *her* songs, and for a while, she lost her voice and felt blue.

But then she found a vocal coach who helped her sing again. . . .

At last, Cyndi sang her words, her *truth* . . . and got a record deal!

After all the ups and downs of her life, Cyndi was determined to use her voice to connect to others.

She sang an anthem . . . for her mother, for her nana . . . and for her sister, Ellen.

Cyndi's voice rang out around the world.

She let everybody know that it was okay for girls to *wanna have fun* and believe in themselves. She gave permission for women like her mom to follow their dreams. Across the airwaves, Cyndi's music spread love, acceptance, and understanding.

From the stage, Cyndi saw a colorful mass of people bopping and singing along to her songs.

She sang for the kids who didn't quite fit in. She gave them a home in her music. She let them know that *if they were lost, they could find her*. . . .

She sang in gratitude for people like Bob, her art teacher, who helped her along the way.

For these friends, and for everyone, she sang to let them know . . .

not to be afraid . . .
how to show their true colors . . .
that they are beautiful . . .
and that they are all rainbows.

GIRLS JUST WANT TO HAVE FUN
1
CYNDI LAUPER
TIME AFTER TIME
2
CYNDI LAUPER

AUTHORS' NOTE

"Be creative and be yourself and your emotions—your color!"—Cyndi Lauper

Pop icon Cyndi Lauper is a legendary singer and songwriter, an artist who has always forged her own path, and an activist who uses her incredible voice to help others.

Cyndi was born Cynthia Ann Stephanie Lauper in 1953 in Queens, New York. From the very beginning, Cyndi was on a mission to find her true colors as an artist. Life wasn't easy for Cyndi, but she was fortunate to find allies along the way who believed in her and encouraged her to use her talents to the fullest: her mother, Catrine; her grandmother, Concetta; her sister, Ellen; her art teacher, Bob Barrell; and her friends in Vermont and New York. Long before there were cheering crowds, these special people made sure Cyndi knew that she was loved and supported.

In 1983, Cyndi Lauper lit up the music scene with her debut album, *She's So Unusual*. Suddenly, Cyndi was everywhere . . . on the radio, on MTV, and singing live in concerts all over the world. Her first single, "Girls Just Want to Have Fun," went straight to number one on the record charts. In 1985, Cyndi won the Grammy for Best New Artist, and in 1984, she was awarded Best Female Video at the first-ever MTV Video Music Awards! In 1986, Cyndi's second album, *True Colors*, came out to rave reviews. The title song, "True Colors"—a ballad about self-acceptance and appreciating one another's differences—became an instant classic. All these years later, Cyndi is still recording music and has sold over fifty million records worldwide!

Cyndi has used her voice in other powerful ways. In 2008, as an ally to the LGBTQIA+ community, she founded True Colors United, a nonprofit organization dedicated to ending homelessness among LGBTQIA+ youth. In 2011, Lauper helped open the True Colors Residence, a thirty-bed shelter in Harlem, New York, for LGBTQIA+ youth; a second location, True Colors Bronx, opened in 2015.

"It's hard to live in the cold. I lucked out. I'm not there. But it doesn't mean I forgot and that I can't help."—Cyndi Lauper

Cyndi also supports women's rights, and HIV/AIDS and mental health awareness, using her platform to speak out for what she believes in and to inspire others to do the same. The Human Rights' Campaign recognized her activism with the National Equality Award in 2005, and she received the United Nations Human Rights' first-ever High Note Global Prize in 2019. Cyndi was even a special guest at President Obama's second inauguration!

Cyndi also wrote the original score for the Tony Award–winning musical *Kinky Boots* and penned a best-selling memoir. In everything she does, Cyndi lets her true colors shine through and encourages others to do the same.

"People can save the world by the way they think and by the way they behave and what they hold to be important."—Cyndi Lauper

Facing page: Cyndi through the years: 1970 *(top left)*, 1983 *(bottom left)*, 1984 *(top right)*, 2006 *(bottom right)*

For art teachers, especially Mrs. J!
—A. G.

For C + C, as always. For Beth and Suzanne, my personal '80s icons
—J. T.

For Lila
—B. B.

ATHENEUM BOOKS FOR YOUNG READERS • An imprint of Simon & Schuster Children's Publishing Division • 1230 Avenue of the Americas, New York, New York 10020 • The text for this book was set in Ruddy. • The illustrations for this book were rendered digitally. • Manufactured in China • 1225 SCP • First Edition • 2 4 6 8 10 9 7 5 3 1 • Library of Congress Cataloging-in-Publication Data • Names: Guglielmo, Amy, author. | Tourville, Jacqueline, author. | Barrager, Brigette, illustrator. • Title: Like a rainbow : the colorful story of Cyndi Lauper / Amy Guglielmo and Jacqueline Tourville ; illustrated by Brigette Barrager. • Description: First edition. | New York : Atheneum Books for Young Readers, 2026. | Audience: Ages 4–8 | Audience: Grades 2–3 | Summary: "A picture book biography of singer and activist, Cyndi Lauper"— Provided by publisher. • Identifiers: LCCN 2024029826 (print) | LCCN 2024029827 (ebook) | ISBN 9781665962001 (hardcover) | ISBN 9781665962018 (ebook) • Subjects: LCSH: Lauper, Cyndi, 1953—Juvenile literature. | Singers—United States—Biography—Juvenile literature. | Sexual minority activists—United States—Biography. | LCGFT: Picture books. • Classification: LCC ML3930.L18 G84 2026 (print) | LCC ML3930.L18 (ebook) | DDC 782.42164092 [B]—dc23/eng/20240628 • LC record available at https://lccn.loc.gov/2024029826 • LC ebook record available at https://lccn.loc.gov/2024029827